INOUE PRESENTS

THE DUKE OF DEATH AND HIS MAID

8

CONTENTS

Chapter 96: Souvenirs

YOUR GRACE.
LEAAAN

GOOD MORNING.

YOU'RE TOO CLOSE!!

YOU DIDN'T SEXUALLY HARASS ME IN TOWN, SO I LOWERED MY GUARD...
IT'S GOOD TO HAVE YOU BACK (?)
BA-DUMP BA-DUMP BA-DUMP
I'M GLAD TO BE BACK.

WE'RE GOING TO GIVE ROB THESE SOUVENIRS WE'VE GOT.

I WONDER IF HE'S STILL ASLEEP.

HE GETS UP LATE ON SNOWY DAYS.

THIS IS THE FIRST TIME IT'S SNOWED IN A WHILE.

ARE YOU COLD?

NO...

I DON'T NEED YOU TO WARM ME UP OR ANYTHING.

THIS MAID'S UNIFORM IS SUR-PRISINGLY WARM, YOU KNOW.

ARE YOU TELLING ME I SHOULD PUT IT ON?!!

FANCY THAT!!

THEY'RE AS CLOSE AS THEY'VE EVER BEEN.

KA-
CHAK
WOW...
ROB'S ROOM IS ALWAYS CRAMMED WITH USELESS STUFF.
IT'S LIKE A CASTLE OF JUNK.
MESSY...

WHO ARE YOU CALLING JUNK?!!
RATTLE
YIKES!!
SORRY!!
DIDN'T KNOW YOU WERE THERE, LI'L OL' POT...

RISE...
MORNING, ROB.

Y-YOUR GRACE.
I'M SO GLAD YOU MADE IT BACK SAFELY...
SOB SOB...
WE TALKED ABOUT THAT YESTERDAY.

POP
ANYWAY...

HOW DID YOU GET ALL THIS STUFF?
RUMMAGE
?
I CAN'T BEAR TO PART WITH ANYTHING I'VE BEEN GIVEN.

I EVEN HAVE A BOOK OF CHILDHOOD DRAWINGS YOU MADE, YOUR GRACE.
HEY, I NEVER GAVE YOU THAT!!

I WANT TO SEE.
I'LL LET YOU HAVE IT, ALICE!
HEY, DON'T GO GIVING AWAY OTHER PEOPLE'S STUFF!!

PLUNK
WE BROUGHT YOU SOME SOUVE-NIRS.
THERE'S EVEN SOME FROM THE FOLKS AT CIRCUS GEMINI.
THE FOLKS AT THE CIRCUS, *HUH?*
THAT WAS NICE OF THEM. WE HAVEN'T EVEN MET.
THESE ARE FROM THE RING-MASTER.
FREE TICKETS TO USE ON OUR NEXT VISIT.
SHFT
Circus Gemini

HERE'S A PAPER CRANE FROM **LUCA.**

AND A BEAR MADE OF BENT NAILS FROM **MEINESZ.**

PEUKERT GAVE YOU SOME WORDS OF ENCOUR-AGEMENT.
HANG IN THERE!

AND JESSIE GAVE YOU THIS SCRAP OF NEWS-PAPER.
TO

HUGO GAVE YOU HIS AUTO-GRAPH.
Hugo

AND HERE'S A CAT-SHAPED ROCK FROM CUFF.
IT'S JUST FOR YOU !!

THEY'RE ALL WON-DERFUL. I LOVE THEM.
A BIG HIT WITH THE OLD GUY
You can peep with this.
Peep at what?
ZAIN GAVE YOU THIS SPY-GLASS.

PERHAPS IT'S GOOD FOR BIRD-WATCHING?
?
WHAT'S THIS?

CAN YOU SEE ANY-THING?
NO, NOTHING.
JUST YOU.

THANK YOU FOR EVERYTHING YOU'VE DONE FOR ME.

IT'S NO TROUBLE...

THANK YOU, ALICE.

I'M SUCH A LUCKY FELLOW.

LET'S PLAY SOME-TIME.
YOU USED TO PLAY CHESS WITH ME A LOT WHEN I WAS LITTLE.
......!!
YES.
LET'S.
I'LL GO MAKE SOME COFFEE.
TH...
THANK YOU.
STEP
SO MANY GOOD THINGS HAVE HAPPENED TO ME TODAY...
I WONDER IF SOMETHING BAD WILL HAPPEN SOON.
DON'T SAY THAT. YOU'LL JINX YOUR-SELF.
ぱたーん
KA-CLUNK
I'M SUCH A LUCKY FELLOW.
I REALLY AM...

THAT NIGHT...
IN ALICE'S ROOM.
FLIP
BA-BA-DUMP
ぎゅっ CLUTCH
SHE SWOONED OVER THE DUKE'S DRAWINGS.
ぱた FLOP

Chapter 97: Going on a Diet

YOU'VE PUT ON SOME WEIGHT, HAVEN'T YOU?
HUH?!
PLUMP

TIGHT
YOU'RE MUFFIN-TOPPING OVER THEM!!
OH, HUSH! YOU'RE TOO LOUD.
TIGHT

LET'S GET YOU SLIM, VIOLA!
YOU'LL RUIN YOUR HEALTH IF YOU GET ANY HEAVIER.
DO YOU HAVE TO LOOK SO SERIOUS?
GRAB
YOU CAN LECTURE ME ABOUT WEIGHT ALL YOU WANT, BUT I DON'T HAVE TO LISTEN.
(LYING BLATANTLY) ROB SAID HE LIKES SLENDER GIRLS.
HEE HEE

OKAY, I'M GOING ON A DIET!!
CLATTER

STRETCH
BESIDES WATCHING WHAT I EAT...
WHAT KIND OF EXERCISES SHOULD I DO?
STRETCH
STRETCH
I'M NO EXPERT, SO I MAY BE GIVING YOU THE WRONG ADVICE...
BUT I THINK YOU SHOULD START WITH SOME STRETCHING.
STRETCH
FOLLOWED BY SOME ANAEROBIC EXER-CISES LIKE WEIGHT TRAINING...
AND THEN AFTER, SOME AEROBIC EXERCISES LIKE WALKING OR RUNNING.
FINISH IT OFF WITH SOME MORE STRETCHES. DO THIS ONCE EVERY OTHER DAY.
SQUEEZE
SQUEEZE
SQUEEZE
OH, SOME OF THE EXTRA WEIGHT WENT TO MY BOOBS!
HEH!
GO AHEAD, SQUEEZE THEM WHILE YOU CAN.
YOU WON'T HAVE THEM FOR LONG.

KICK
THAT'S THE SPIRIT, VIOLA!!
KICKING ME IS ONE WAY TO GET SOME EXERCISE!!
THEY SAY BOXING HELPS TRIM DOWN YOUR WHOLE BODY!!

SO GO AHEAD, PUNCH ME!!
KICK!!
HARDER!!
PUNCH!!
MADAM, LET'S GO OVER THERE.
?

HUFF...
HUFF...
IS THAT THE BEST YOU CAN DO, VIOLA?

I'M SURE YOU CAN DO BETTER IF YOU PRETEND I'M SOMEBODY YOU DESPISE.
YEAH...

BAM
PRETEND I'M FIRST-BORN!!
OMG... DID YOU MAKE THAT MASK?!

LIFT
FIFTEEN.
SIXTEEN.
LIFT
LIFT
WHEW! THESE ARE HEAVY!! SEVEN-TEEN.
WEIGHT TRAINING HAS TO BE THE MOST BORING THING IN THE WORLD.
EIGH-TEEN.
IT MAY BE TOUGH AT FIRST, BUT IT'S FUN ONCE YOU GET USED TO IT.
DON'T SIT IN FRONT OF ME.
AND QUIT STARING.

KRCH
KRCH
THUD
AH, I'M SO TIRED.
YOUR FORM'S BAD.
HOW CAN YOU INSTRUCT PEOPLE IN THE ART OF LOVE WITH SUCH A FLABBY BODY?
PUT SOME HEART INTO IT.
OH, BE QUIET!!
JOG
I CAN'T TAKE ANY MORE OF THIS...
WORN OUT
VIOLA...

Why are you crying, Viola?
Come here.

Mother got mad at me for not being able to play the piano as well as Brother Dearest.
......
It's all his fault.
He's the one to blame.
GRRR...
Walter.

I'll keep practicing until I'm good, so keep me company!!

I LOVE THAT YOU'RE ABLE TO WORK HARD IN SECRET.

KEEP IT UP!!
YOU GOT THIS.
HANG IN THERE...
VIOLA!!

CLENCH...

I SWEAR I'M GOING TO LOSE WEIGHT AGAIN!!

WAAAAHHH!!

CHUCKLE...

ONE MONTH LATER.

I LOST WEIGHT!!

I'LL CELEBRATE WITH SOME MACARONS!!

WOO-HOO!

DON'T GO GAINING IT ALL BACK NOW.

RELAX. THIS MUCH IS NO BIGGIE.

HERE...

YOU CAN HAVE ONE.

THE DUKE OF DEATH
AND HIS MAID

THE DUKE OF DEATH
AND HIS MAID

Chapter 98:
The Staring Contest

THIS HAPPENED ABOUT TWO YEARS AGO...
JUST AFTER ALICE FIRST ARRIVED AT THE DUKE'S VILLA.

CLICK
CLACK

IS THERE SOMETHING I CAN HELP YOU WITH...
YOUR GRACE?
CLICK...

BA-DUMP

THIS IS FRAYED.

I'D LIKE YOU TO MEND IT.

OF COURSE, I'LL TAKE CARE OF IT.

IT'S HOPELESS...

NOW THAT I'VE BECOME AWARE OF ALICE'S PRESENCE...

BA-DUMP

BA-DUMP

BA-DUMP

BA-DUMP

BA-DUMP

I CAN'T STOP STAMMERING.

I BET SHE THINKS I'M A CREEP.

I WISH I WAS DEAD.

TH... THANKS.

LEAAAN...
YOUR GRACE.
YOU SHOULD LOOK PEOPLE IN THE EYES WHEN YOU SPEAK TO THEM.
ペタ
STUCK LIKE GLUE
WHAT ARE YOU DOING?
I CAN'T.
I GET NERVOUS.

OKAY, THEN...

WHY DON'T YOU LOOK AT MY CHEST INSTEAD?

BOING!!

THAT'S EVEN WORSE!!

WHY DO PEOPLE HAVE TO LOOK EACH OTHER IN THE EYES WHEN THEY SPEAK?

MUMBLE MUMBLE MUMBLE MUMBLE

ISN'T HAVING A CONVERSATION GOOD ENOU WHY MAINT EYE CONTACT

SHALL WE PRACTICE TALKING?

P... PRACTICE?

YOUR GRACE...

LOOK AT ME, PLEASE.

BA-DUMP BA-DUMP BA-DUMP BA-DUMP BA-DUMP BA-DUMP BA-DUMP BA-DUMP

I CAN'T.

WE WON'T BE ABLE TO PRACTICE, THEN.

HOW ABOUT WE HAVE A STARING CONTEST INSTEAD?
WE'LL BOTH MAKE A STRANGE FACE. THE FIRST ONE TO SMILE LOSES.
HUH?!
THIS IS A STARING CONTEST.
HUH? HUH?
YOU SMILE, YOU LOSE.
APPUPPU.
POUFF!

YOU MUSTN'T LOOK AWAY SO QUICKLY.
LET'S TRY AGAIN.
DO WE HAVE TO?
THIS IS A STARING CONTEST.
YOU SMILE, YOU LOSE.

APPUPPU!
PUFF!
SHE JUST MADE THE SAME FACE.
PLEASE DON'T BREAK EYE CON-TACT.
GRIN
LET'S TRY AGAIN.
THIS IS A STARING CONTEST.
YOU SMILE, YOU LOSE.
I...
LOVE YOUR EYES, YOUR GRACE.

THEY HAVE A WARMTH TO THEM...
IT'S BEEN THERE SINCE WE WERE LITTLE.

PLEASE LET ME SEE MORE OF THEM.

......
BA-DUMP
BA-DUMP
BA-DUMP
BA-DUMP

GLANCE

EYES MEET

HEY...
YOU KNOW WHAT?
ALICE HAS GORGEOUS EYES.
I WISH I COULD LOOK INTO THEM LONGER...
STARE...
SMILE
YOU FINALLY LOOKED AT ME.
OH, DEAR.
I SMILED THIS TIME, SO I LOST.
I FORGOT ALL ABOUT THE STARING CONTEST.
I THINK IT'S TIME I CUT MY HAIR...

Chapter 99: A Date at the Zoo

LOVE
OH!
THEY KISSED.

DID YOU SEE THAT, HUGO?!
EXCITED
EXCITED
EXCITED

ZAIN, COME OVER HERE.
GUYS...

YEAH!!
IT WAS SO CUTE.

YOU DO KNOW WHY WE'RE HERE, RIGHT?
TO HAVE A GOOD TIME!!
TO LOOK FOR NEW RECRUITS!!

ONE HOUR AGO.
I'D LIKE YOU TO GO SCOUT NEW RECRUITS FOR CIRCUS GEMINI.
GO DO IT YOURSELF.
YOU CAN GO ON A DATE WITH CUFF AT THE SAME TIME.
JUMP
I'M GOING TOO!!
STARE
I'M WATCHING YOU! DON'T TRY ANY FUNNY BUSINESS WITH HER!!

CHATTER
Welcome!!
ZOO
CHATTER

YAWN...

THERE'S A GOOD-SIZED CROWD HERE.
IF I SPOT SOMEONE PROMISING, I'LL ASK THEM TO JOIN OUR TROUPE.
BEAM

ANYHOO, THIS IS THE FIRST TIME CUFF AND I HAVE GONE OUT SINCE WE STARTED DATING. HOW UNROMANTIC CAN YOU GET?
THIS IS SUPPOSED TO BE A DATE, RIGHT?
LOOKING AT ANIMALS IS BORING...

SPARKLE SPARKLE...

WELL, MAYBE IT'S NOT THAT BAD...
ZAIN PREFERS LOOKING AT GIRLS.

MR. CIRCUS BIRD!!

SQUEEZE...

GRIN

LET'S LOOK AT THE ANIMALS TOGETHER, ZAIN.

OKAY. ♥
ZAIN'S ON CLOUD NINE.

CAN I GIVE YOU A HUG?
STOP RIGHT THERE, YOU SEX FIEND!!
WE'RE OFF TO THE NEXT EXHIBIT!!

DON'T LOOK AT CUFF WITH THOSE LECHEROUS EYES.
HEY!
BUT I'M HER BOY-FRIEND.
STOP RIPPING INTO ME OVER EVERY LITTLE THING.
I ENCOURAGED YOU TO CONFESS YOUR TRUE FEELINGS, REMEMBER?!
GUYS!
AND I THANK YOU FOR DOING THAT.

ZAIN!! IT'S A LION!!
I HEAR THEY'RE CALLED THE KING OF BEASTS.
YOU SURE KNOW YOUR STUFF, CUFF.
ガヤ
YAK
EH HEH HEH.
ガヤ
YAK...
LION
ガヤ
YAK
ガヤ
YAK...

CHATTER
CHATTER

......
CHATTER
わい
CHATTER
わいわい

ひょい
HOIST
THERE! YOU CAN SEE IT NOW, EH?

LIFT ME UP. I WANNA SEE, TOO!!

YOU KNOW, GIVING GIRLS PIGGY-BACK RIDES IS REAL KINKY.

YOU SURE YOU WANT ME TO?

THANKS, ZAIN!!

LIONS ARE SO COOL!!

ROARRRR!!

I HAVE A GREAT IDEA.

HOW ABOUT WE GET A LION FOR CIRCUS GEMINI?

I BET IT'LL BECOME OUR MAIN ATTRACTION.

I DON'T KNOW IF WE COULD ACTUALLY GET OUR HANDS ON ONE...

BUT I BET THE RINGMASTER WOULD BE OPEN TO THE IDEA.

I KNOW HE WOULD.

OK

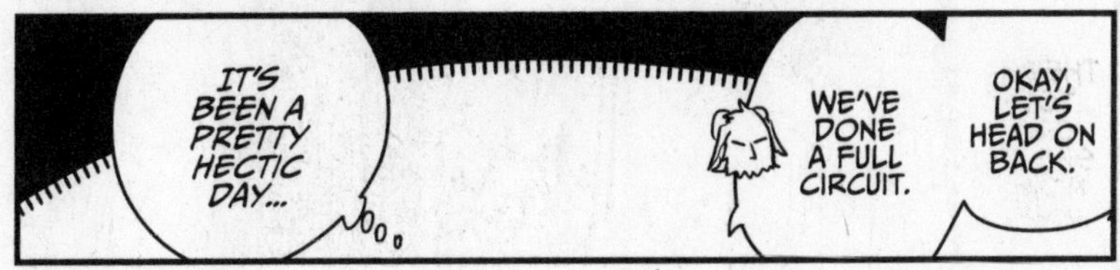

OKAY, LET'S HEAD ON BACK.
WE'VE DONE A FULL CIRCUIT.
IT'S BEEN A PRETTY HECTIC DAY...

THIS WAS SUCH A FUN DATE.

CAN I GIVE YOU A KISS?

NO.

LET ME SQUEEZE YOUR BOOBS?

RUINING A GOOD THING... THAT'S ZAIN'S STYLE.

Chapter 100: Your Boyfriend

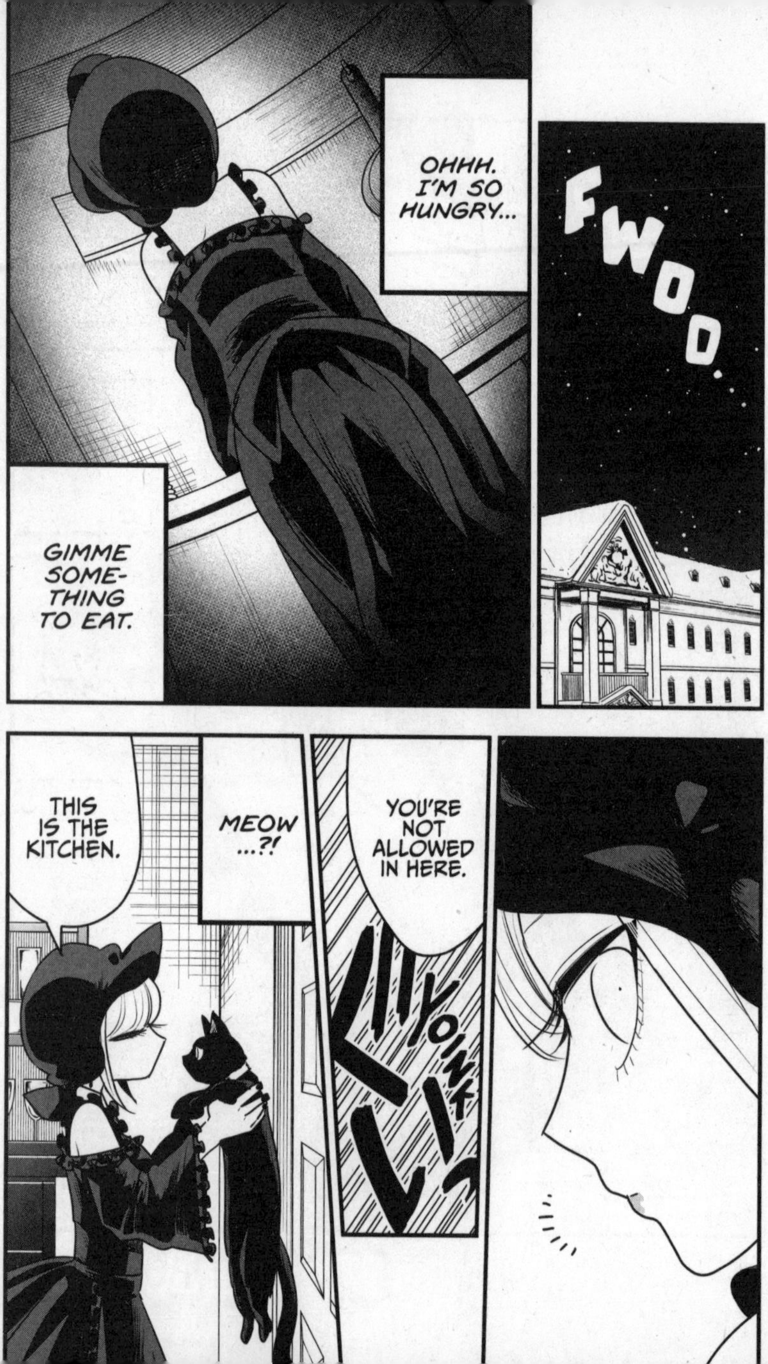

FWOOD.

OHHH. I'M SO HUNGRY...
GIMME SOME-THING TO EAT.

YOINK
YOU'RE NOT ALLOWED IN HERE.
MEOW ...?!
THIS IS THE KITCHEN.

I'LL GIVE YOU SOME FOOD LATER.
KA-CLUNK

KA-CHAK

GIMME IT NOW!!
I'M A CAT!!
MEOWWW MEOWWW!!
IF YOU REALLY CARE ABOUT ME, GIMME SOMETHING TO EAT.

OHH. IT FEELS SO GOOD TO GET PETTED. ♥
PET PET PET PET
PET PET PET PET
PET ME SOME MORE! ♥

KA-CLUNK
TSK.
SHE DIDN'T DO WHAT I ASKED.

SIGH...

Meoww.
HEY, SISSY!!
GIVE THIS POOR CAT SOME-THING TO EAT.
YIKES!!
OH, IT'S JUST A CAT...

INCHES BACK...

SOB...
SOB...
IT'S GOT ME COR-NERED...
THAT'S WHERE YOU WERE TO BEGIN WITH.

GOOD...

ROLL...

ROLL

YOU LIKE PLAYING WITH THAT.

THIS IS LOADS OF FUN.

THE DUKE'S ROLLED-UP NECKTIE

BECAUSE...
I WANT ALICE AND ME TO BE ONE, TOO.

BUT I DON'T HAVE THE RIGHT TO BE HER BOYFRIEND.
THAT'S WHAT'S BEEN BOTHERING ME.

LICK
SORRY, I CAN'T REALLY RELATE.
I'M JUST A CAT.
LICK

ARGHHHH...
TUMBLE
I ONLY WANT TO MAKE HER HAPPY!!
ARGHH!
BUT I CAN'T BECAUSE OF THIS CURSE!!
I'M SUCH A LOST CAUSE.
ARGHH!
THIS GUY'S FREAKING OUT...

I LOVE HER.

SIGH...

I LOVE HER SO MUCH.
I CARE ABOUT HER MORE THAN ANYTHING ELSE.
THAT'S WHY I WANTED TO BE HER SPECIAL SOMEONE.

......

WHAT'S THE MATTER, YOUR GRACE?
SURPRISE!!
ALICE!!
DINNER'S READY, YOUR GRACE.

I FIXED A LITTLE SOMETHING FOR YOU TOO, KITTY.

!!

ALL RIGHT!

CLICK

CLACK

UM, ALICE...

.....

CHOMP

?

I WAS JUST THINKING ABOUT...

HOW MUCH I WANT TO BE YOUR BOYFRIEND.

......

FIFTEEN MINUTES LATER.
ALL IS BACK TO NORMAL.
MMM, DELICIOUS!!

I CAN'T KEEP UP WITH THESE TWO.
MUNCH
MUNCH

THE DUKE OF DEATH
AND HIS MAID

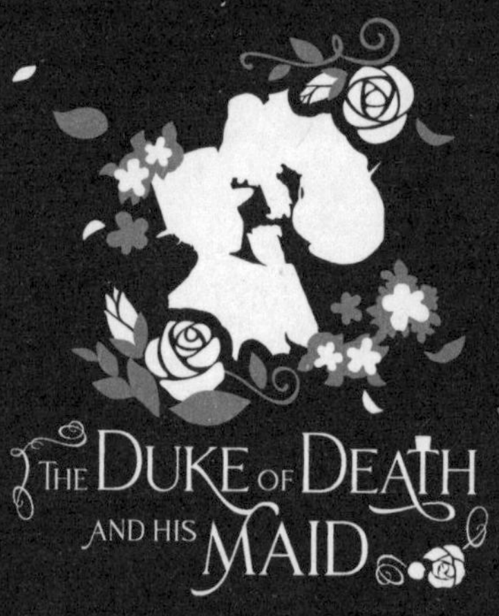
THE DUKE OF DEATH
AND HIS MAID

Chapter 101: The Blizzard

OOOOOO

AW, MAN...

TODAY IS NOT OUR DAY.

WHO WOULD'VE THOUGHT WE'D GET CAUGHT IN A BLIZZARD?

NOW WE CAN'T GO VISIT ALICE AND THE OTHERS.

THE TROUPE MUST BE WORRIED ABOUT US. LET'S HEAD BACK TO TOWN AFTER THIS CLEARS UP.

HERE. WHY DON'T YOU PUT THIS ON...?
NO THANKS.
SLIIP
I'M NOT REALLY THAT COLD.

?
SOAKED

YOUR TOP IS TURNING SEE-THROUGH FROM ALL THE WET SNOW.
MIND IF I TAKE A PEEK?
HOW ABOUT NO?
IT'S FINE. I'LL JUST DRY MYSELF WITH FIRE MAGIC.

FOOMP
CRACKLE
CRACKLE

IT'S BEEN A WHILE SINCE WE'VE BEEN ALONE LIKE THIS.
YEAH.
WE'RE ALWAYS WITH HUGO OR SOMEONE ELSE FROM THE TROUPE...

OO...
オォ
IT'S OUR FIRST NIGHT ALONE AS A COUPLE...
OO...
オォ

CUFF THOUGHT IT COULD BE KIND OF ROMANTIC.

ZAIN THOUGHT IT COULD GET STEAMY.

ZAIN.
WHY DON'T WE DO SOMETHING WE CAN ONLY DO ALONE?
RISE

HUH?!
LIKE GET NASTY?!
NO. YOU WANT TO GET SLAPPED?
GO EASY ON ME, OKAY...?

DOODLE

GUESS WHAT THIS ANIMAL IS.

OH, I REMEMBER...
WE USED TO PLAY THIS OFTEN WITH OUR MAGIC.
THAT'S A FOX.
YEP.

AND THIS IS A CAT.
AND THAT ONE'S ALICE.

OW!
DON'T TOUCH IT. IT'S MADE OF FLAMES, AFTER ALL.

IF ANYTHING HAPPENS, I'LL PROTECT YOU WITH MY MAGIC. SO DON'T WORRY, OKAY?
BUT I'M PROTECTING YOU, REMEMBER?
OH. THEN I'LL PROTECT EVERYONE ELSE.

DO YOU REGRET USING YOUR TIME-CONTROLLING MAGIC?
THUMP
THUMP

NO.
I'VE BEEN THINKING LATELY THAT...

I COULD GO BACK TO BEFORE WHAT'S-HIS-NAME GOT CURSED...
WHAT'S-HIS-NAME
AND USE MY MAGIC TO ALTER HIS FUTURE.

OUR PARENTS COULDN'T AVOID THEIR OWN DEMISE. THEY WERE DESTINED TO DIE.
IT SEEMS FATE IS BEYOND MY CONTROL.

BUT IF HIS CURSE WASN'T PREORDAINED, I JUST MIGHT HAVE A SHOT.
PREOR-WHAT? USE SMALLER WORDS.

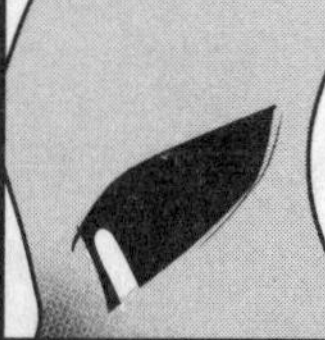
THERE ARE A LOT OF COMPLICATIONS WITH THAT PLAN, BUT THERE'S ONE I DREAD THE MOST.

AND THAT'S GOING TOE TO TOE WITH DALETH'S SISTER.
I'M NOT SURE IF WE CAN WIN AGAINST THE TOUGHEST AND BADDEST WITCH IN THE WORLD.

I'LL POWER UP BEFORE THEN, SO WE'LL BE FINE.

BEEEEAM!

YOU'RE SO DEPEND-ABLE, I COULD ALMOST CRY.
CAN I GIVE YOU A KISS?
NO.

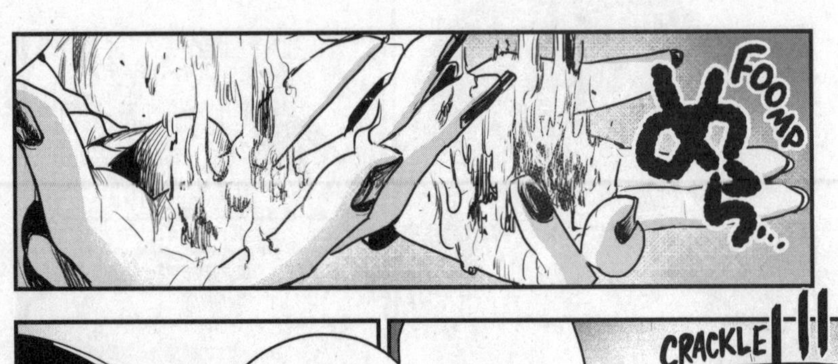
FOOMP
めら…

CRACKLE
ボ…
I WANT TO BREAK THAT CURSE QUICKLY.
THEY'RE MY DEAR FRIENDS, AFTER ALL.

I ALSO WANT TO FIND A WAY FOR THE RINGMASTER TO SEE HIS WIFE AGAIN.
I'LL GIVE THAT SOME THOUGHT, TOO.
WE'LL REPAY ALL THEIR KINDNESS IN THE END.

HEY, ZAIN.

WHAT WOULD YOU DO IF THIS BLIZZARD NEVER STOPS AND WE'RE STUCK HERE FOREVER?

DON'T BE SILLY.

IT'LL CLEAR UP BY TOMORROW AND WE'LL HEAD BACK TO TOWN.

FWOOOOOOOO

ビョオオオオオオオッ

THE NEXT DAY.

SHINE

SHINE

ZAIN, WAKE UP!

THE SUN'S OUT.

SHINE

SHINE

WHY'D THE WEATHER HAVE TO CLEAR UP?

すく

RISE

LET'S FLY BACK.

SMOOCH!

WHAT WAS THAT FOR?

I DON'T KNOW WHEN WE'LL BE ALONE NEXT TIME, SO...

SO IT'S OKAY FOR YOU TO KISS ME BUT NOT FOR ME TO TOUCH YOU?

WHAT, YOU DIDN'T LIKE THAT?

NO. IN FACT, I HOPE YOU'LL DO IT AGAIN.

Chapter 102: Younger Brother and Older Brother

THMP THMP
THMP...

WITH THIS MAGIC ROBE I BOUGHT OFF A MERCHANT...
A MIRROR, AND A FEW MAGICAL PHRASES, I SHOULD BE ABLE TO ATTEND THE WITCHES' SABBATH.
RUSTLE

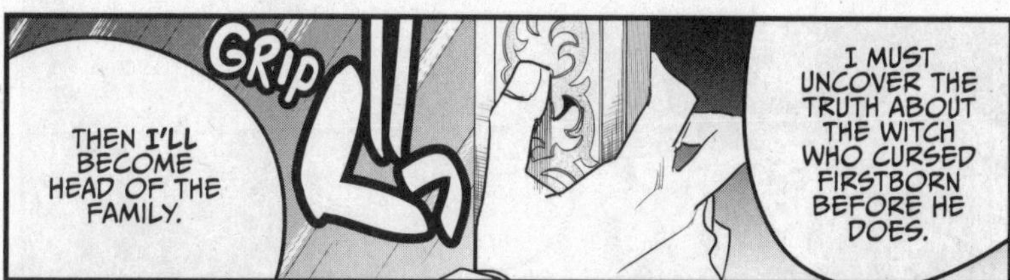

I'LL OUTDO HIM...

I'LL PROVE TO MOTHER THAT I'M MORE THAN JUST SOME SPARE!

YOU'RE GOING TO THE WITCHES' SABBATH AGAIN...?
O O O...

IN THAT OUTFIT?!
THEY ALREADY KNOW WHAT I LOOK LIKE. I MIGHT AS WELL DRESS LIKE A WITCH THIS TIME.

WHAT DO YOU THINK?
YOU LOOK CUTE. LIKE THE SUM OF ALL EARTHLY CUTE-NESS...

DON'T YOU FEEL UNEASY GOING WITHOUT CUFF AND ZAIN?

I'LL USE THIS ROCK.

THE ONE CUFF GAVE ROB.

PULL

THAT'S A PRETTY SEXY PLACE TO KEEP IT.

HSS

GLUB

CUFF LIKELY CARRIED IT CLOSE TO HER ALL THE TIME...

SO IT STILL HAS TRACES OF HER MAGICAL POWER.

ARE YOU COMING OR NOT, YOUR GRACE?
I'M PERFECTLY FINE GOING BY MYSELF.

OF COURSE I'M COMING!!
I CAN'T LET YOU GO ALONE.

......
YOU'RE SUCH A GENTLE-MAN. ♥

A GENTLE... HUH?!
HEY, THIS IS ZAIN'S SPYGLASS...
GLUB

JUMP
WAIT FOR ME!

WALTER, MEAN-WHILE...
SNEAK

CREEP

SPOOKY WITCH WORLD
HA HA HA HA HA HA HA...
AGHHHH...
わい CHATTER
KEE KEE KEE KEE...
FLAP FLAP
わい CHATTER

DALETH'S, LIKE, SO NOT LEAVING HER CHURCH.

WE, LIKE, TOTALLY CAN'T START THE SABBATH WITHOUT HER.

SIGHHHHH.

SOMEONE SAW HER FACE. SEEMS SHE'S TAKING IT PRETTY HARD.
SO, WITCHES DO HAVE A LEADER.
GUESS I'D BETTER HEAD OVER TO THE CHURCH.
THAT RICH KID IN THE TOP HAT IS, LIKE, GRODY TO THE MAX!
!!

I COULD, LIKE, NEVER GET ALONG WITH A PANSY LIKE HIM!!
FIRST-BORN?!
I KNOW WHAT YOU MEAN, BIKINI GIRL.
JUST LIKE ME.

THE ENEMY OF MY ENEMY IS MY FRIEND.
THUMBS UP!
ARE YOU ALL RIGHT?
YIKES...

Y...YOU SCARED ME...
YOU WERE WAY TOO CLOSE TO ME...

ASHEN...

W...

WALTER !!

COME BACK HERE!!

CHARGE

Chapter 103: Younger Brother and the Maid
PLEASE FALL ASLEEP WITH (A PILLOW OF) ME IN YOUR ARMS.
?!

TREAD
HIS GRACE TOLD ME TO STAY WITH YOU, LORD WALTER...
SO I CAN'T GO BACK.
I GET PRETTY TENSE AROUND GIRLS.
TREAD
TREAD
I'D APPRECIATE IT IF YOU'D JUST LEAVE ME ALONE.

ALICE, WAS IT?
ARE YOU CONTENT WITH BEING FIRSTBORN'S SERVANT?
IT'S NOT RIGHT FOR A GIRL LIKE YOU TO BE COOPED UP IN A MANSION IN THE WOODS.

ACTU-ALLY...
I'M HAPPY TO SPEND MY DAYS BY HIS GRACE'S SIDE.

SERI-OUSLY?
HE'S NOT THAT GREAT A GUY.
YOU JUST DON'T UNDERSTAND HIM, LORD WALTER.

HE'S YOUR OLDER BROTHER, SO YOU HAVE SIMILAR PERSONALITIES.
I BELIEVE YOU TWO COULD GET ALONG.
WHOA, NOW!!

THE STRAIGHT MAN'S...
GONE. SO...
THE FUNNY WOMAN...
AND...
THE PSYCHOPATH...
CONTINUE...
WALKING THROUGH THE MIST.

DA- DA- ドォ
DA- DUM... オオ...

TRICK OR...
(GIMME A TREAT...)

SMIRK
TREAT?
(OR I'LL PLAY A TRICK ON YOU.)

I'M SORRY, I DON'T HAVE ANY TREATS...

YANK

DASH
KEH KEH.
MY PENDANT...

TRIP

OW...
THAT HURTS.
GIVE HER THAT PENDANT BACK.
ROLL ROLL ROLL ROLL ROLL

HEY!!
I HEARD WHAT YOU SAID BACK THERE!!
POINT
YOU'VE GOT A COMPLEX! SECOND BORN, SECOND PLACE!
NYAH, NYAH!! MR. RUNNER-UP!!

I DON'T KNOW WHAT YOU'RE TALKING ABOUT.

IT'S WRITTEN ALL OVER YOUR FACE!!

DASH

HEY!!

COME BACK HERE!!

CAN YOUR PENDANT BE FIXED?
YES.
WHAT'S MORE IMPORTANT TO ME IS THE PHOTOGRAPH INSIDE.

LET'S GET IT BACK.
OFF
SLIPS
HERE, PUT THIS ON.

IT'S A WITCH'S ROBE.
TOSS
IT KEEPS WITCHES FROM KNOWING YOU'RE HUMAN.
YOU SHOULD WEAR IT, LORD WALTER.
I'LL BE FINE.

WHY ARE YOU BEING SO NICE TO ME?

YOU'RE A GIRL, SO I HAVE TO PROTECT YOU.

CREEEAK!

IF SHE WERE A GUY, HE'D LET HER FEND FOR HERSELF.

YOU'RE SO SWEET.

JUST LIKE HIS GRACE...

BLARGH!

......
SORRY.
THUD
TO BE CONTINUED.

Chapter 104: Two Younger Brothers

PREVIOUSLY...
WALTER AND ALICE CAME TO RETRIEVE HER PENDANT.

OOO...

CREEEAK...

WHY, YOU LITTLE ...!!

SCAMPER

THINK YOU CAN RUN AND HIDE IN THE BACK?

NYAH, NYAH!! STUPID SECONDBORN!!
BLEH!!
JUST TRY AND CATCH ME!

コッ
CLACK

SORRY FOR MAKING YOU GO THROUGH ALL THIS TROUBLE.
CLICK
CLACK
WHEN I CATCH HIM, I'M GIVING HIM A GOOD TALKING-TO.
THAT KID NEEDS TO BE TAUGHT A LESSON.

......
しん
SILENCE
WHERE IS HE...?

I REMEMBER...
WHEN I WAS A KID.

FIRSTBORN WAS BAD AT HIDE-AND-SEEK.
HEE HEE...
HE WAS ALWAYS SO EASY TO FIND.

I, ON THE OTHER HAND, WOULD HIDE IN TIGHT SPACES WITHOUT MOVING A MUSCLE.
BA-DUMP
BA-DUMP
I COULD HIDE FOR HOURS AND NOT BE FOUND. SOME-TIMES THEY FOR-GOT ALL ABOUT ME.
GIDDY
GIDDY

IT'S ALL FIRSTBORN'S FAULT.
GRR...
HUFF!
HUFF!
HUFF!
......

I KNOW YOUR GAME!! YOU'RE MAKING US THINK YOU'RE IN THE CLOSET...
BUT YOU'RE ACTUALLY BEHIND IT!!
YOU SHOULD LOSE SOME WEIGHT!!
UH-OH!
THUD
SQUEEZE
SQUEEZE
HOP

HERE I AM!!
NYAH, NYAH!! SECOND-BORN!!
DARN... HOW'D YOU GET OVER THERE?
IS THERE A SECRET PASSAGE SOME-WHERE?

I'M NOT BACKING DOWN IN A FIGHT!!
I'LL BEAT YOU A SEXDE-CILLION TIMES OVER!!
DASH
HE KNOWS SOME RATHER LARGE NUMBERS.

ARE YOU A SECOND-BORN?
POP
SECOND-BORNS? MORE LIKE SUCKER-BORNS!

IT SEEMS...
TP
TP
WE'RE AT A DISAD-VANTAGE AS LONG AS WE'RE IN THIS HOUSE.
TP

AGRHHHHH!!
BONK
LORD WALTER...
MAXIMUM STRESS.

HUFF!
HUFF!
DEEP BREATH...

I NEED TO CALM DOWN...
AND KEEP OBSERVING.

ALL THIS STRESS IS FIRSTBORN'S FAULT...
ALL OF IT.
HUH...?
WALTER'S JUST TAKING IT ALL OUT ON THE DUKE.

TREAD
I'M...
DONE CHASING YOU.
HUFF!
OH, GIVING UP AL-READY?
YOU'RE SUCH A LOSER, SECOND-BORN.
KEH KEH KEH
KEH!
THERE ARE TWO OF YOU.
YOU'RE BROTHERS WHO LOOK EXACTLY ALIKE...
AND YOU'RE THE YOUNGER OF THE TWO.

IT'S OKAY TO STAND UP FOR YOURSELF.

THAT'S WHAT SIBLING RIVALRY IS ALL ABOUT.

I FOUND HIS BROTHER.
YAAANK
YOINK

ALL RIGHT, HAND OVER THE PENDANT.
NO WAY!!

RUMMAGE

HERE YOU GO!!
THANK YOU.

SLAP
SLAP
SLAP
SLAP
SLAP
THANK YOU FOR GETTING MY PENDANT BACK.

IT'S VERY DEAR TO ME.
LORD WALTER MIGHT JUST BE...
KINDER THAN I THOUGHT.
NO PROBLEM.
THMP
THMP
THMP
THMP
WHAT I WANT TO KNOW IS...

WHY DID IT HAVE TO BE TWO OF YOU...?
I HATE THAT NUMBER. GET ANOTHER SIBLING...
OR THREE.
TREMBLE
TREMBLE
LET'S GO TO THE CHURCH.
I'M WORRIED ABOUT HIS GRACE.
NEXT TIME, THEY'RE OFF TO THE CHURCH!!

Chapter 105:
Younger Brother and
Younger Sister

オオオ
OOO...

ARE YOU REALLY CLIMBING YOUR WAY IN, LORD WALTER?
IT'S SAFER THAN SNEAKING THROUGH THE FRONT DOOR.

I'LL COME GET YOU IF THE COAST IS CLEAR.
IF ANYTHING HAPPENS, CALL OUT TO ME.

よじ...
CLIMB
よじ...
CLIMB

HE'S SUCH A MAN OF ACTION.
OOO
よじ...
CLIMB

I'M DONE FOR.

THEY SAW IT.

MY HIDEOUS FACE.

Dear Daleth. Your face looks exactly like mine. It's ever-so confusing.

Why don't I **change** it so people can tell us apart?

I HATE YOU, BIG SISTER.

IT'S YOUR FAULT MY LIFE'S A MESS.

I KNOW EXACTLY HOW YOU FEEL!!

FLINCH!!

RAISE

WHO GAVE YOU PERMISSION...

TO ENTER MY CHURCH?

LIFT

YANK

IT'S FUNNY TO THINK I'D SYMPATHIZE WITH A WITCH...
BUT I ALSO HAVE IT TOUGH BECAUSE OF AN OLDER SIBLING.
COUGH
JUST LIKE YOU.
COUGH...

WHO...
WHO ARE YOU?
AND WHY ARE YOU HERE?
GETS UP
MY NAME'S WALTER.

I CAME HERE TO TRY TO LEARN MORE ABOUT MY BROTHER'S CURSE.
I WAS PLANNING TO SPY ON YOU.

BUT I SAW A LADY WEEPING.

FLUSTER

M...

LADY? HOW PRETENTIOUS.

MY FACE IS ALL SCARRED UP. HIDEOUS.

YOU'RE HANDSOME. YOU WOULDN'T UNDERSTAND.

MY LOOKS DON'T MATTER. I CAN'T BECOME HEAD OF MY FAMILY.

YOU'RE BEAUTIFUL.
HAVE MORE CONFI-DENCE IN YOURSELF.

DAAA-LETH!!
SORRY TO BARGE IN ON YOU WHEN YOU'RE, LIKE, FEELING DOWN!!
BWAM!!

WE, LIKE, CAUGHT OURSELVES A COUPLE RATS!!
PLUNK

GASP!

......

COVER

SOB SOB SOB...

S-SORRY!! I KNOW YOU, LIKE, HATE PEOPLE SEEING YOUR FACE...

I'M NOT HIDING IT ANY LONGER.

THIS IS HOW I'LL BE FROM NOW ON.
WHOAAAA...
CLAP CLAP
CLAP
CLAP

CLAP CLAP
CLAP

CLAP
CLAP CLAP
CLAP CLAP

THE DUKE AND ALICE HAVE NO IDEA WHAT'S UP, BUT DECIDED TO ROLL WITH IT.

Chapter 106: Younger Sister and Older Sister

DALETH RELEASED THE DUKE AND ALICE...
AND DISMISSED THE OTHER WITCHES.
BUMMED
WALTER !!
RUN
ARE YOU ALL RIGHT?!
SHUT UP, SCUM !!
I'LL TAKE THAT AS A "YES."
WHOOSH
SHF

COME WITH ME.
I HAVE SOME-THING TO SHOW YOU.

THIS COULD BE A TRAP...
CHICKEN.
THAT'S WHY YOU'RE NOT FIT TO BECOME THE HEAD OF THE FAMILY.

FOLLOW
HE'S LESS THAN A CHICKEN. MORE OF A MAGGOT.
HEY, THAT'S GOING TOO FAR!
FOLLOW

......
I HATE TO ADMIT IT, BUT I'VE STILL GOT A LOT TO LEARN ABOUT PEOPLE.
YOU'VE GOT WAY MORE COURAGE THAN I DO.

I WISH I COULD LET YOU BECOME THE HEAD OF THE FAMILY.
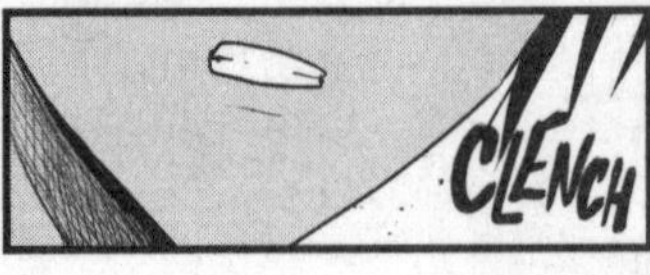
CLENCH

"LET ME BECOME," YOU SAY...?
QUIVER QUIVER
GNASH GNASH
YIKES...

DID I SAY SOMETHING WRONG?
WALTER'S COMPLETELY RIGHT, YOU KNOW.
AREN'T YOU BEING ODDLY EASY ON HIM?!

YOU KNOW WHAT?!! I REALLY DO DESPISE YOU!!
I'VE GOT TO BECOME HEAD OF THE FAMILY OR IT'S ALL POINTLESS!!
SPITTLE

FIRST, I'LL BREAK YOUR CURSE...
THEN I'LL PUNCH YOUR LIGHTS OUT!!
HUFF! HUFF!
HUFF!
HUFF!
NOW THAT'S JUST PLAIN MEAN.

THEN FIGHT BACK.
IT'S TIME WE HAD SOME SIBLING RIVALRY.

......

MAYBE I SHOULD'VE FOUGHT BACK...
AND NOT OBEYED HER ALL THE TIME...

"WE'RE THE SAME," HE SAYS.
AND HE'S RIGHT.

WHY DOES THIS HUMAN CHILD HAVE THE POWER TO MOVE ME?

YOU'RE BEAUTIFUL...
BEAUTIFUL...
(ECHO)

I'VE BEEN CELIBATE FOR OVER 150 YEARS. I CAN'T TAKE THIS MUCH EXCITEMENT.
MUMBLE
ボソ…
HE'D BETTER TAKE FULL RESPONSIBILITY FOR THIS...
?
LITTLE DOES WALTER KNOW THAT SOMEONE INCREDIBLY HIGH-MAINTENANCE HAS FALLEN FOR HIM.

ギギ!!
CREAK...
ギギ!!
CREAK...

WHAT TERRIBLE DECOR.

WHAT'S IN THERE? A MUMMY?
OH, YOU HUSH.

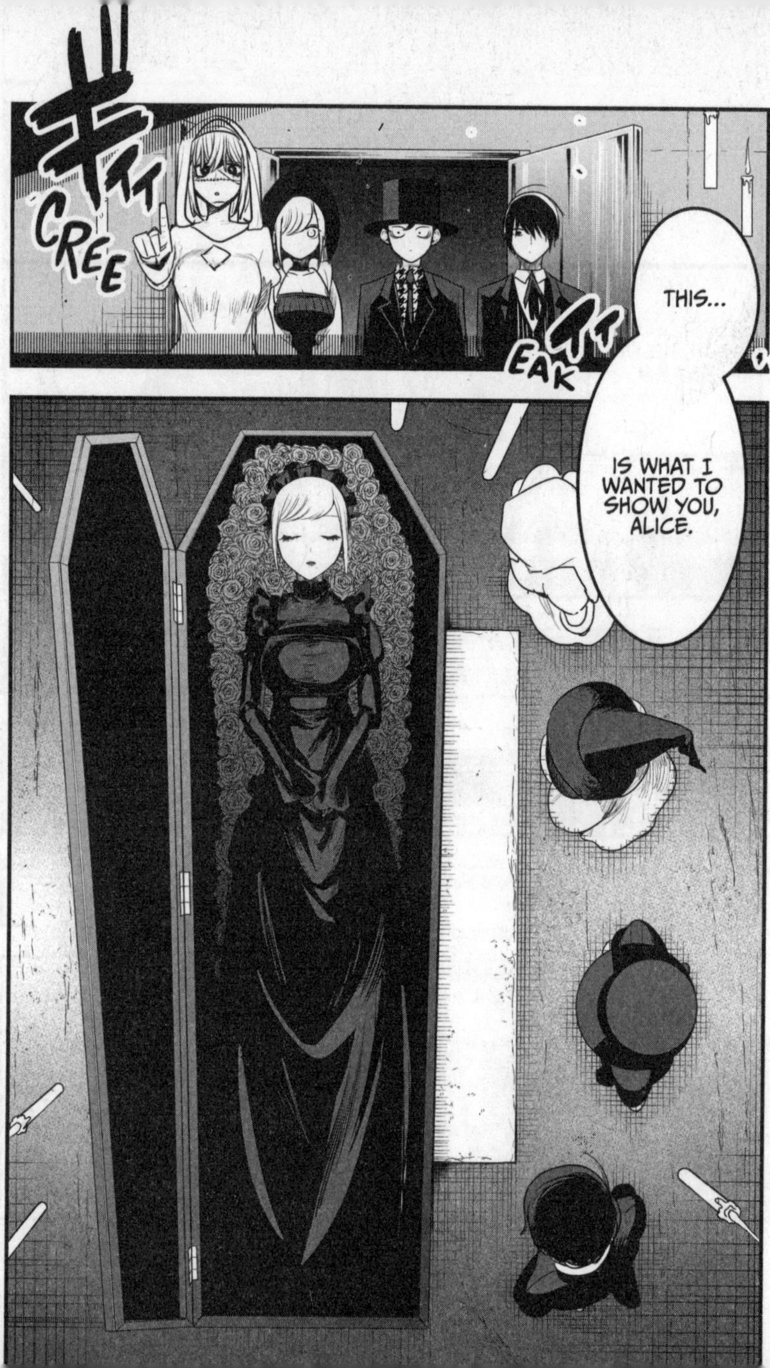

CREE

EAK

THIS...

IS WHAT I WANTED TO SHOW YOU, ALICE.

AS I TOLD YOU BEFORE, SHARON LIVES.
BUT THAT'S...

I MAY BE A MEAN OLD WITCH, BUT THIS IS NEITHER A LIE NOR AN ILLUSION.
PINCH YOUR CHEEKS AND SEE FOR YOUR-SELF.
PINCH

そっ
SHF

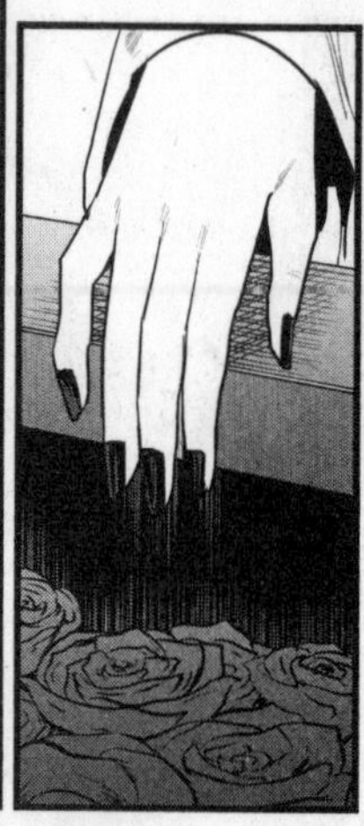

LUB-
DUB

MOTHER...
MOTHER.
SHE'S IN A COMA.
MY SISTER CURSED HER.

LUB-
DUB
...!!
LUB-
DUB
LUB-
DUB

EVEN I DON'T KNOW WHY SHE DIED.

I THOUGHT SHARON MIGHT KNOW SOMETHING. THAT'S WHY I WANT TO REVIVE HER.

BESIDES, I WAS QUITE FOND OF HER.

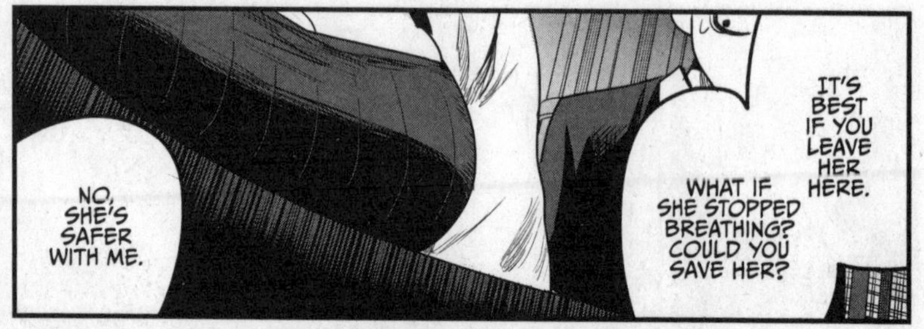
IT'S BEST IF YOU LEAVE HER HERE.
WHAT IF SHE STOPPED BREATHING? COULD YOU SAVE HER?
NO, SHE'S SAFER WITH ME.

YOU'RE RIGHT. YOU'VE LOOKED AFTER HER FOR OVER A DECADE.
PLEASE CONTINUE TO TAKE GOOD CARE OF HER.
I PROMISE I'LL COME BACK FOR HER.

WAIT FOR ME, MOTHER.

DALETH ...

PLEASE TELL US WHAT HAPPENED AT THE MAIN HOUSE.

Chapter 107: Mother and Daughter

WELL, THEN...

WHAT DO YOU WANT TO KNOW?

TELL US EVERYTHING.

EVERY SINGLE THING YOU KNOW ABOUT MY CURSE.

SUCH A SPOIL-SPORT...

FOR NOW, COULD YOU TELL US WHAT HAPPENED AT THE MAIN HOUSE?

OH, ALL RIGHT...

SNAP

FOR WALTER'S SAKE, I'LL GIVE YOU GUYS A HINT.

WHOA!!

IT'S THE MAIN HOUSE.

IT'S AN ILLUSION, STUPID.

RUN
TREAD
THIS IS THE MAIN HOUSE AS IT WAS JUST BEFORE YOU WERE CURSED.
HEY, WHO ARE YOU CALLING A DOUBLE-BAGGER? YOU GOT A DEATH WISH?
BUT NOBODY SAID ANY-THING...
TREAD

YOU'RE TOO SLOW, LITTLE BROTHER AND SISTER!!
RUN
WAIT FOR US, BIG BROTHER!!

SINCE THIS IS AN ILLUSION, I CAN MAKE YOU THE FIRST-BORN.
THANKS...
BUT IT DOESN'T REALLY HELP MUCH.

FLAP
FLAP
FLAP...

HEY, SHARON!!

WHAT'S ALICE UP TO TODAY?
RUSTLE
AH, ALICE?
BA-DUMP
THAT'S MOTHER'S VOICE.
BA-DUMP
SHE'S RESTING IN HER ROOM.

POINTS...

AND MY SISTER'S OVER THERE...

HER NAME'S SADÉ.
THE SHADY-LOOKING CHARACTER BEHIND HER IS ME.
RUSTLE RUSTLE RUSTLE
SO THAT'S THE WITCH WHO CURSED ME...
SHUDDER
SHE'S LOOKING AT SHARON...

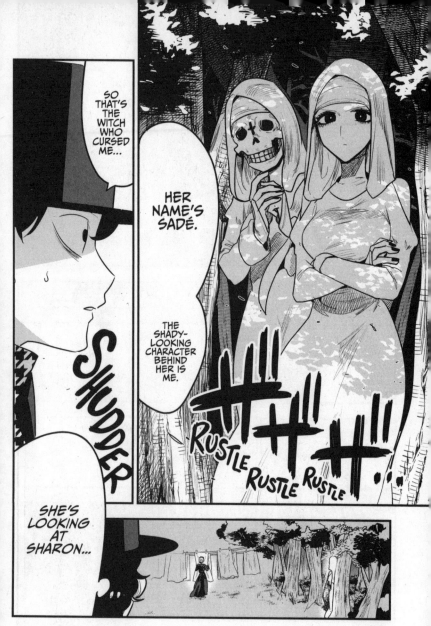

HER EYES ARE FRIGHT-ENING...
THEY'RE FILLED WITH SUCH HATE.
SHUDDER...

I'VE SEEN ENOUGH.
YOU CAN DISPEL THE ILLUSION.
PAT
THANK YOU, WALTER.
LEAN
CAN I VISIT YOU ONCE IN A WHILE?
?
SURE, I DON'T MIND.

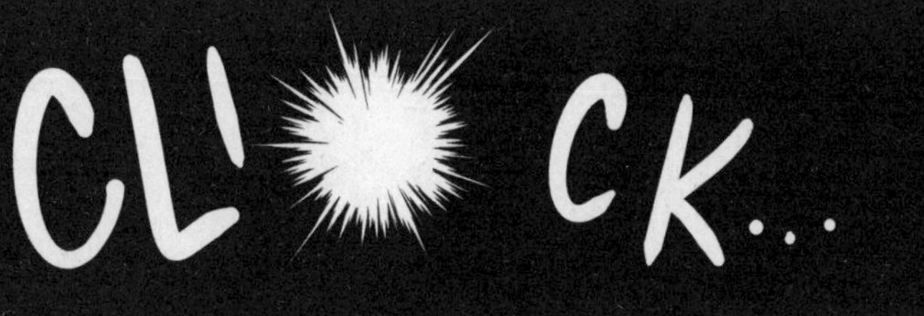
CLICK...

AWAKENS
UHHH...
WHERE ARE WE...?

THE VILLA.
IT SEEMS WE WERE FORCIBLY TELEPORTED BACK.
I SEE...
TIGHT
HER BOOBS ARE PRAC-TICALLY SPILLING OUT OF HER TOP...
TIGHT

HE'S INCREDIBLE.
HE'S GOT THIS VITALITY THAT'S ON A WHOLE OTHER LEVEL.
I HOPE HE MADE IT BACK TO THE MAIN HOUSE ALL RIGHT.
FRANKLY, WE ONLY LEARNED SO MUCH BECAUSE WALTER WAS WITH US.
SIGH...

WAH HA HA HA HA HA!

GAWD, WHAT A CREEP.
HEY, VIOLA! SHOW ME MORE RESPECT!
JOT JOT JOT JOT JOT
I'M STEADILY GETTING CLOSER TO BEING THE HEAD OF THE FAMILY!

THE DUKE OF DEATH
AND HIS MAID

THE DUKE OF DEATH
AND HIS MAID

Chapter 108: Shopping

YOO-HOO! LITTLE MISS VIOLA HERE.
I CAME TO TOWN TODAY TO SEE CUFF'S CIRCUS.
SHWIP
Circus Gemini
VIOLA ALWAYS MAKES HER BUTLERS WAIT OUTSIDE.
CLICK
CLACK
I THINK CUFF'S LOOKING AFTER THE NEW LION WE GOT.
CLICK
REALLY?

IT'S TAKEN A LIKING TO HER...AND BECOME QUITE A HANDFUL.
KA-CHAK
YOO-HOO, CUFF!! HOW ARE YOU DOING?

CHOMP
ばくっ
SHE'S DEAD!!
HEY, VIOLA!!
THRILLED
YOU CAME.
ぱた
KICK
ぱた
KICK
JUST WAIT, I'LL BE OUT IN A SECOND.
DON'T LOOK!!
じた
WRIGGLE
じた
WRIGGLE

SCHLOOP

SORRY TO KEEP YOU WAITING.

WHY IS SHE SO HOPELESSLY GOOD-LOOKING?!

WE'VE GOT SOME TIME BEFORE THE SHOW STARTS. LET'S HAVE SOME FUN OUTSIDE.

OOO, LET'S GO SHOPPING!

I THINK CUFF'S TAKEN A SHINE TO ME.

IT'S BEEN AGES SINCE I WAS LAST IN TOWN.

GIDDY

GIDDY

I'VE ALWAYS GOT LESSONS AND STUFF, SO I RARELY GET OUT OF THE HOUSE.
IT'S GREAT TO BE ABLE TO HANG OUT WITH A FRIEND LIKE THIS.
GASP!

I'M ONLY HERE TO KEEP YOU COMPANY, CUFF!!
DON'T GET THE WRONG IDEA OR ANYTHING!!
FLUSTERED
FLUSTERED
WARM FUZZIES
VIOLA, YOU REALLY BLOW HOT AND COLD, DON'T YOU?

I'LL PICK OUT SOME-THING NICE FOR YOU!!
JUST LEAVE EVERYTHING TO ME AND MY AWESOME FASHION SENSE.
BOUTIQUE
CLANG
CLANG
THANKS, I APPRECIATE IT.
YOU KNOW, ZAIN USUALLY PICKS OUT EVERYTHING IN MY WARDROBE.

TICK
TOCK
HAVE YOU GOT IT ON YET?
NOPE.
RUSTLE
RUSTLE
VIOLA!!
SWISH

POKE...

HELP ME PUT IT ON.
WHIMPER...
WHIMPER...

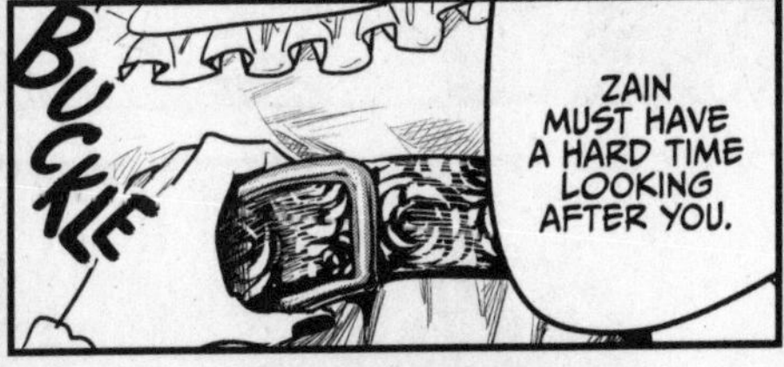
ZAIN MUST HAVE A HARD TIME LOOKING AFTER YOU.
BUCKLE

YEAH, HE DOES.
I'M REALLY GRATEFUL FOR HIM.
OKAY, BELT'S ON. YOU'RE GOOD TO GO.

WHOA...
THIS IS NICE.
FRILLY
FRILLY
YOU'VE GOT GREAT TASTE.

YOU SHOULD GO INTO THIS LINE OF WORK.

THERE'S NO WAY I COULD DO THAT.

I'M A MEMBER OF THE NOBILITY, REMEMBER?

TRY IT FIRST, AND THEN DECIDE.

AFTER I PAY FOR THIS, LET'S HEAD BACK TO THE CIRCUS!!
THE SHOW WILL START SOON!!
I'LL BLOW YOU A KISS IF I SPOT YOU IN THE AUDIENCE!!
WAG
WAG
OKAY, OKAY...

YAAAAAY...
CLAP
CLAP
CLAP
I DON'T KNOW WHY, BUT...
UNDER THE SPOTLIGHT'S GLOW, CUFF'S LIKE A TOTALLY DIFFERENT PERSON.

SHE SPARKLED...

LIKE EVERYONE'S FAVORITE STAR.

SHE'S SO COOL.

EYES MEET

MWAH!

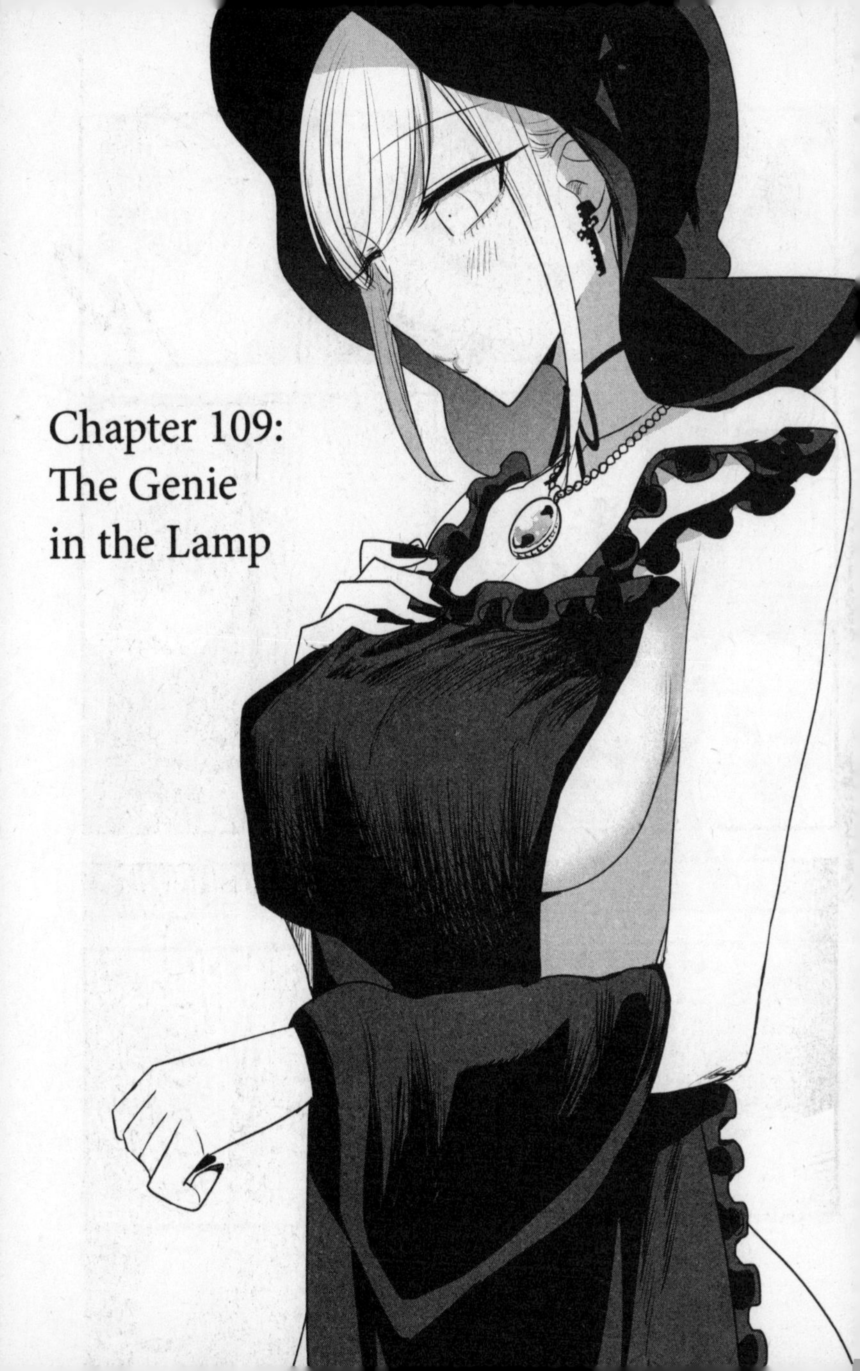
Chapter 109:
The Genie
in the Lamp

WHAT'S THAT...?

AND WHAT'S IT DOING SITTING ON YOUR CHEST?
WHAT DO YOU THINK IT IS?

SOME DODGY MAGICAL ITEM THAT ZAIN GAVE YOU...
SMILE
BINGO!

STARE
STARE
STARE
STARE

IT'S JUST A PLAIN OLD LAMP.
HE SAID YOU'VE GOT TO RUB IT FOR IT TO WORK.

SO, GIVE IT A RUB.
NICE AND HARD. ♥
WHY ARE YOU TALKING INTO MY EAR...?

RUB RUB RUB RUB
COULD THIS BE A MAGIC LAMP...
WITH A GENIE THAT'LL GRANT ME THREE WISHES?
PUFF
PUFF
PUFF

GENIE OF THE LAMP, COME TO ME!!

YOU SUMMONED ME, HUMAN?

HAZY

TURN

ALICE...

DID YOU START A PART-TIME JOB?!

THE DUKE'S CONFUSED.

NO, YOU ARE MISTAKEN.

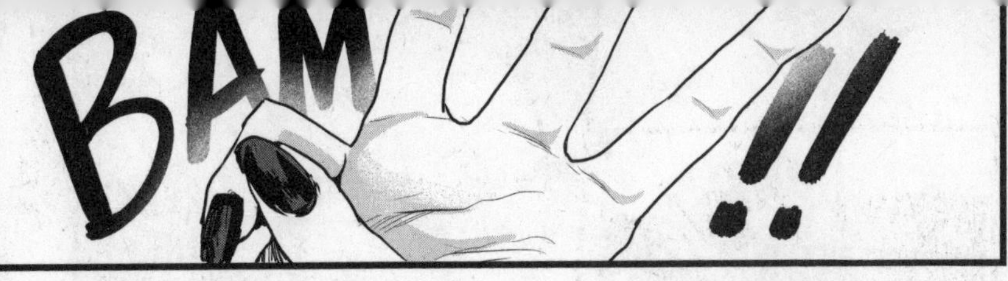
BAM!!

TELL ME YOUR THREE WISHES...
AND I SHALL GRANT THEM.

WHEN YOU TALK, IT SOUNDS LIKE ALICE IS SPEAKING ROUGHLY TO ME. IT KINDA TURNS ME ON.
WILL YOU GRANT ANYTHING I WISH FOR?
THAT WAS NOT MY INTENTION.

I ALREADY KNOW WHAT I'M GOING TO WISH FOR.

BREAK THE CURSE ON ME!!
VERY WELL.
YOU MEAN, YOU CAN DO IT?!

FLOAT
FLOAT

I SHALL PROVE IT TO YOU.
THIS WILL BE YOUR SECOND WISH.
POOF

FLOAT...

BWOOF
IT DIDN'T WITHER ...!!

GLANCE
TH...
THAT MEANS ...

......

I CAN TOUCH ALICE?!

BUT THE CURSE WAS TOO POWERFUL TO COMPLETELY DISPEL.
SO I TRANSFERRED IT TO SOMEONE ELSE.

NO...I DON'T BELIEVE IT.
THERE'S GOT TO BE SOME KIND OF CATCH.
THERE IS NO CATCH.

WHAT...?!
I FORCED SOMEONE SOMEWHERE TO BEAR THE CURSE.

ASHEN...

SO NOW SOMEONE ELSE HAS TO SUFFER BECAUSE OF IT...?!
WAAH!
YOU ARE CORRECT.

BUT IT IS NO LONGER *YOUR* PROBLEM.
ISN'T THAT ALL THAT MATTERS?

NOW, TELL ME YOUR FINAL WISH.

!...

ARE YOU SURE THAT'S WHAT YOU WANT-ED?
TO HAVE THE CURSE PUT BACK ON YOU?
I DON'T WANT ANYONE TO SUFFER JUST SO I CAN BE HAPPY.
I'M SURE I WOULD REGRET IT LATER ON.

IT'S FINE. I WASN'T EXPECTING MUCH FROM THE MAGIC LAMP TO BEGIN WITH.
YOU'RE ALWAYS SO THOUGHTFUL, YOUR GRACE.
THANKS. YOU'RE TOO CLOSE, THOUGH.

REST

SHE LOOKED REALLY GOOD IN THAT EXOTIC ATTIRE.
THAT'S WHAT THE DUKE CHOSE TO REMEMBER.

THE PERSON WHO UNWITTINGLY RECEIVED THE DUKE'S CURSE.
THE SPROUT SUDDENLY SHRIVELED UP...
WITHER
HAVE I FINALLY GAINED SOME SPECIAL POWERS ...?

Chapter 110: The Kiss

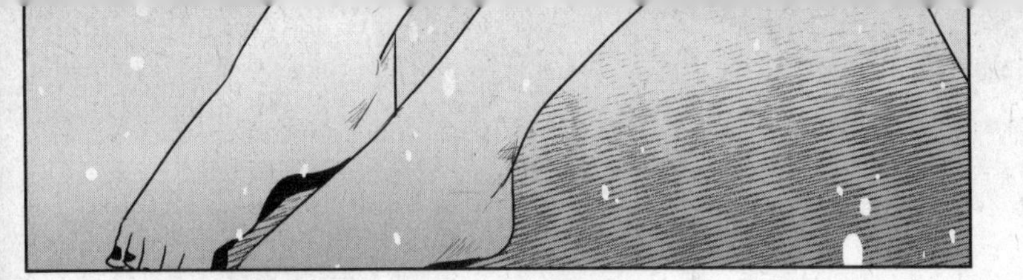

SPLASH...

Cuff and Zain...
When did you start dating?!
Who asked who out first?!
CHATTER
CHATTER
Now, Jessie...
......

Have you kissed yet?!

WAH HA HA!

Ummm...

Well...

you see...

You're like an open book...

Aww, that's so cute! ♡

You guys kissed! ♡

GRIN GRIN

OH, GOD!

Do you have to talk so loud?!

AFTER-WARDS.
I THINK I'M GOING TO TURN IN FOR THE NIGHT.
ALL RIGHT, YOUR GRACE.
DAB
DAB
DAB
DAB
DAB
PRESS
......

DO YOU WANT SOME TOO, YOUR GRACE?

N-NO THANKS!!

TH-THAT'D BE LIKE AN INDIRECT KISS!

I'LL GIVE YOU A NEW ONE, OF COURSE.

HIDE

I WISH THERE WAS A HOLE I COULD CRAWL INTO.

OR WOULD YOU RATHER USE MINE?

HEE HEE HEE...

QUIT TEASING ME.

YOU DON'T HAVE TO WALK ME TO MY ROOM.
I WANT TO, SO DON'T MIND ME.

EVEN THOUGH WE'LL SEE EACH OTHER TOMORROW, I STILL MISS YOU WHEN YOU GO.
I HATE IT WHEN WE PART.

THEN THINK OF ME WHEN YOU DO *IT* TONIGHT.

?!!

WRITE POETRY, THAT IS.

……

IF I STAY OUT ANY LONGER, I MIGHT CATCH A COLD, SO I'M GOING INSIDE.
GOOD NIGHT, ALICE.
GOOD NIGHT, YOUR GRACE.

ザク CRUNCH
ザク CRUNCH

ザリ ザク CRUNCH
ザリ ザク CRUNCH

CRUNCH...

GLANCE
......

ALICE?
WHAT IS IT? DID YOU FORGET TO TELL ME SOMETHING?
EXHALE
KNOCK
KNOCK

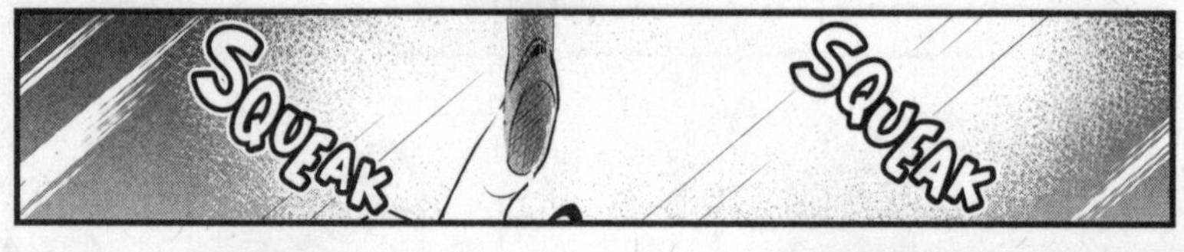
SQUEAK
SQUEAK

?
Kiss me

THEIR HEARTS WERE BEATING SO FAST...
THEY FORGOT HOW COLD THE WINDOWPANE WAS.

The Duke of Death and His Maid Vol. 8 · End

THE DUKE OF DEATH
AND HIS MAID

THE DUKE OF DEATH
AND HIS MAID

Bonus Chapter

TA-DA
I'M DONE!!
I WROTE ZAIN AND THE OTHERS A LETTER.
I'M GOING TO GIVE IT TO THE MAIL CARRIER.
SO IT ISN'T A LOVE LETTER, THEN.
WHY WOULD I WRITE THEM A LOVE LETTER?
I'D LIKE YOU TO WRITE ME ONE.
BA-DUMP
I COULD WRITE A WHOLE BOOK ABOUT...
HOW ADORABLE YOU ARE, ALICE!!
OH MY...! HEE HEE HEE.

WHAT'S THIS...?
YOUR GRACE, ARE YOU STUDYING?
CLICK
CLACK
LOVE LETTERS TO ALICE.
YEAH, UH-HUH. (NOPE!)
SCRIBBLE SCRIBBLE SCRIBBLE
YOU'RE STUDYING WITHOUT BEING TOLD TO.
FLIP
I FEEL LIKE I'M WATCHING YOU GROW WITH EACH PASSING DAY.
IT'S SO TOUCHING I COULD CRY...
HEY!
DON'T WIPE YOUR TEARS WITH THAT!!

CUFF, LET'S MAKE A SAUNA WITH YOUR MAGIC.
DOES A SAUNA TASTE GOOD?
WHIRL
NO, IT'S SOME-THING FUN.

I WANT YOU TO MAKE THE ROOM HOTTER.
SWEAT
ALL I NEED TO DO IS USE MY FLAMES TO MAKE IT HOTTER?!
PRETTY MUCH.

THE RESULT.
ABLAZE

SOME-THING'S NOT QUITE RIGHT...
ARE WE HAVING FUN YET?

ZAIN AND THE RINGMASTER AT 3 A.M.
EXHALE...
HOW ARE THINGS WITH YOU AND CUFF THESE DAYS?
PRETTY MUCH THE SAME.
4 A.M.
THE LION'S GOING TO JOIN US ON STAGE IN A WEEK.
I'VE GOT A BAD FEELING ABOUT IT.
SIGH...
CLINK
YOU'RE SMARTER THAN I AM, SO DON'T SWEAT IT.
5 A.M.
YOU HAVEN'T SEEN YOUR WIFE IN TEN YEARS. DON'T YOU EVER WANT TO HOOK UP WITH ANOTHER GIRL?
OTHER GIRLS DON'T INTEREST ME.
DON'T YOU EVER GET HORNY?
6 A.M.
I CAME TO COLLECT HIM.
ZZZ
DRAPES JACKET
YOU'RE A LUCKY GUY TO BE DATING CUFF, ZAIN.

CUFF LOOKED SPECTACULAR BACK AT THE CIRCUS.
SIGH...

GASP...
WHY DO I GET ALL MUSHY WHEN THINKING ABOUT HER?!!
ARGHHH!
CLICK
CLACK

SOME-THING ON YOUR MIND, VIOLA?
PAT
SCRAM!

YOU SPARE!! SECOND-BORN!! TWO TWO TWO TWO!!
ARRGGHHH!!
BLAAAAAST
DON'T SAY THOSE WORDS JUST TO GET RID OF ME!!
HEH.

ALL RIGHT!!
I'M OFF TO SEE ALICE!!
A SELECTION OF HIS FAVORITE PAGES.
IT'S GREAT THAT YOU TWO GET ALONG SO WELL.

I LOVE HER, THAT'S WHY.
YOU MUST'VE LOVED SOMEONE AT SOME POINT, ROB, RIGHT?
CLICK
CLACK
I'VE BEEN A BUTLER FOR SO LONG, I'VE NEVER LOVED ANYONE OR BEEN IN A RELATIONSHIP.

YOU NEVER MENTIONED THAT.
DOES THAT MEAN YOU'VE NEVER KISSED ANYONE BEFORE?!
OH, YOUR GRACE, YOU'RE SO INNOCENT.
HUH? HE'S SUDDENLY BECOME ALL GROWN-UP ON ME...

End of Bonus Chapter

THE DUKE OF DEATH
AND HIS MAID

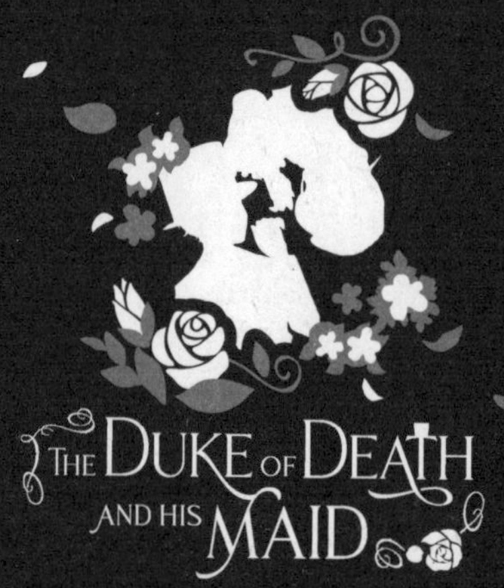
THE DUKE OF DEATH
AND HIS MAID

HAVE YOU EVER SEEN A STRING TELEPHONE, YOUR GRACE?
WITH THIS, I CAN SPEAK WITH YOU FROM A DISTANCE.
WOW, THE WONDERS OF MODERN TECHNOLOGY!

AS AN EXPERIMENT, I'LL TRY TALKING TO YOU FROM THE OTHER ROOM.
KA-CLUNK
ALL RIGHT.

MUMBLE
MUMBLE
MUMBLE

DID YOU MAKE OUT WHAT I WAS SAYING?
KA-CHAK
SOMETHING I CAN'T REPEAT IN PUBLIC.
THEN IT WORKED!

SEVEN SEAS ENTERTAINMENT PRESENTS

story and art by INOUE VOLUME 8

TRANSLATION
Josh Cole

ADAPTATION
John Ramirez

LETTERING
Aila Nagamine

ORIGINAL COVER DESIGN
Yasuo Shimura (siesta)

COVER DESIGN
H. Qi

PROOFREADER
Dave Murray

EDITOR
K. McDonald

COPY EDITOR
B. Lillian Martin
Matthew Birkenhauer

PRODUCTION DESIGNER
Christina McKenzie

PRODUCTION MANAGER
John Ramirez

PREPRESS TECHNICIAN
Melanie Ujimori
Jules Valera

MANAGING EDITOR
J.P. Sullivan

EDITOR-IN-CHIEF
Julie Davis

ASSOCIATE PUBLISHER
Adam Arnold

PUBLISHER
Jason DeAngelis

SHINIGAMI BOCCHAN TO KURO MAID Vol. 8
by INOUE

Original Japanese edition published by SHOGAKUKAN.
English translation rights in the United States of America, Canada, the United Kingdom, Ireland, Australia and New Zealand arranged with SHOGAKUKAN through Tuttle-Mori Agency, Inc.

Seven Seas press and purchase enquiries can be sent to Marketing Manager Lianne Sentar at press@gomanga.com. Information regarding the distribution and purchase of digital editions is available from Digital Manager CK Russell at digital@gomanga.com.

ISBN: 979-8-88843-012-5
Printed in Canada
First Printing: September 2023
10 9 8 7 6 5 4 3 2 1

READING DIRECTIONS

This book reads from ***right to left***, Japanese style. If this is your first time reading manga, you start reading from the top right panel on each page and take it from there. If you get lost, just follow the numbered diagram here. It may seem backwards at first, but you'll get the hang of it! Have fun!!

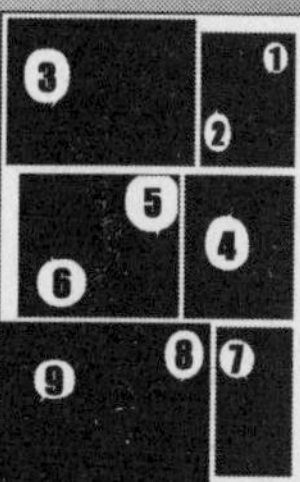

Follow us online: www.SevenSeasEntertainment.com

INOUE

Me and the cat at
my parents' house are
inseparable.